W0009638

DOVER · THRIFT · EDITIONS

# The Rubáiyát of Omar Khayyám

### FIRST AND FIFTH EDITIONS

# EDWARD FITZGERALD

DOVER PUBLICATIONS, INC.
*New York*

# DOVER THRIFT EDITIONS

## EDITOR: STANLEY APPELBAUM

Published in Canada by General Publishing Company, Ltd.,
30 Lesmill Road, Don Mills, Toronto, Ontario.
Published in the United Kingdom by Constable and Company, Ltd.

This Dover edition, first published in 1990, is an unabridged
and unaltered republication of the first and fifth editions of *The
Rubáiyát of Omar Khayyám.* (Original editions published by Bernard
Quaritch, London: first edition, 1859; fifth edition, 1889.) A new
Notes section has been prepared specially for the Dover edition.

Manufactured in the United States of America
Dover Publications, Inc.
31 East 2nd Street
Mineola, N.Y. 11501

*Library of Congress Cataloging-in-Publication Data*

Omar Khayyam.
[Rubā'īyāt.  English]
The Rubaiyat of Omar Khayyam / [translated by] Edward FitzGerald.
Translation of : Rubā'īyāt.
p.   cm. — (Dover thrift editions)
"This Dover edition, first published in 1990, is an unabridged and
unaltered republication of the first and fifth editions of The Rubaiyat
of Omar Khayyam. (Original editions published by Bernard Quaritch,
London: first edition, 1859; fifth edition, 1889)"—T.p. verso.
ISBN 0-486-26467-X (pbk.)
I. FitzGerald, Edward, 1809–1883.   II. Title.   III. Series.
PK6513.A1   1990
891'.5511—dc20                          90-37716
                                        CIP

# Note to the Dover Edition

OMAR KHAYYAM (ca. 1048–1122) was a Persian mathematician, astronomer and philosopher who was not known as a poet in his lifetime. Later a constantly growing corpus of *rubaiyat* (quatrains), largely skeptical and hedonistic in nature, became attached to his name, though only some of them were genuinely his work.

In 1859, Edward FitzGerald (1809–1883), a well-educated English country gentleman who also did translations from Spanish and ancient Greek, published a free adaptation of a selection of this Persian poetry, creating what was essentially a new work of English poetry. This anonymous publication (FitzGerald's authorship was not revealed until 1875) became so popular after its discovery by D. G. Rossetti and others that revised and expanded editions appeared in 1868, 1872 and 1883. The fifth edition, published posthumously in 1889, was based on FitzGerald's handwritten changes (mainly affecting punctuation) in a copy of the fourth edition.

The present volume includes the complete text of the first and fifth editions. The fifth edition has become one of the best-known and most often quoted pieces of English writing. A brief new Notes section, explaining Persian names and unfamiliar terms, has been added at the end of this Dover edition.

# Contents

# Text of the
# First Edition
## *(1859)*

**1**

Awake! for Morning in the Bowl of Night
Has flung the Stone that puts the Stars to Flight:
    And Lo! the Hunter of the East has caught
The Sultán's Turret in a Noose of Light.

**2**

Dreaming when Dawn's Left Hand was in the Sky
I heard a Voice within the Tavern cry,
    "Awake, my Little ones, and fill the Cup
"Before Life's Liquor in its Cup be dry."

**3**

And, as the Cock crew, those who stood before
The Tavern shouted—"Open then the Door!
    "You know how little while we have to stay,
"And, once departed, may return no more."

**4**

Now the New Year reviving old Desires,
The thoughtful Soul to Solitude retires,
    Where the WHITE HAND OF MOSES on the Bough
Puts out, and Jesus from the Ground suspires.

### 5

Irám indeed is gone with all its Rose,
And Jamshýd's Sev'n-ring'd Cup where no one knows;
   But still the Vine her ancient Ruby yields,
And still a Garden by the Water blows.

### 6

And David's Lips are lock't; but in divine
High piping Péhlevi, with "Wine! Wine! Wine!
   *"Red* Wine!"—the Nightingale cries to the Rose
That yellow Cheek of hers to incarnadine.

### 7

Come, fill the Cup, and in the Fire of Spring
The Winter Garment of Repentance fling:
   The Bird of Time has but a little way
To fly—and Lo! the Bird is on the Wing.

### 8

And look—a thousand Blossoms with the Day
Woke—and a thousand scatter'd into Clay:
   And this first Summer Month that brings the Rose
Shall take Jamshýd and Kaikobád away.

**9**

But come with old Khayyám, and leave the Lot
Of Kaikobád and Kaikhosrú forgot!
    Let Rustum lay about him as he will,
Or Hátim Tai cry Supper—heed them not.

**10**

With me along some Strip of Herbage strown
That just divides the desert from the sown,
    Where name of Slave and Sultán scarce is known,
And pity Sultán Máhmúd on his Throne.

**11**

Here with a Loaf of Bread beneath the Bough,
A Flask of Wine, a Book of Verse—and Thou
    Beside me singing in the Wilderness—
And Wilderness is Paradise enow.

**12**

"How sweet is mortal Sovranty!"—think some:
Others—"How blest the Paradise to come!"
    Ah, take the Cash in hand and waive the Rest;
Oh, the brave Music of a *distant* Drum!

### 13

Look to the Rose that blows about us—"Lo,
"Laughing," she says, "into the World I blow:
    "At once the silken Tassel of my Purse
"Tear, and its Treasure on the Garden throw."

### 14

The Worldly Hope men set their Hearts upon
Turns Ashes—or it prospers; and anon,
    Like Snow upon the Desert's dusty Face
Lighting a little Hour or two—is gone.

### 15

And those who husbanded the Golden Grain,
And those who flung it to the Winds like Rain,
    Alike to no such aureate Earth are turn'd
As, buried once, Men want dug up again.

### 16

Think, in this batter'd Caravanserai
Whose Doorways are alternate Night and Day,
    How Sultán after Sultán with his Pomp
Abode his Hour or two, and went his way.

### 17

They say the Lion and the Lizard keep
The Courts where Jamshýd gloried and drank deep;
   And Bahrám, that great Hunter—the Wild Ass
Stamps o'er his Head, and he lies fast asleep.

### 18

I sometimes think that never blows so red
The Rose as where some buried Caesar bled;
   That every Hyacinth the Garden wears
Dropt in its Lap from some once lovely Head.

### 19

And this delightful Herb whose tender Green
Fledges the River's Lip on which we lean—
   Ah, lean upon it lightly! for who knows
From what once lovely Lip it springs unseen!

### 20

Ah, my Belovéd, fill the Cup that clears
TO-DAY of past Regrets and future Fears—
   *To-morrow?*—Why, To-morrow I may be
Myself with Yesterday's Sev'n Thousand Years.

### 21

Lo! some we loved, the loveliest and best
That Time and Fate of all their Vintage prest,
　　Have drunk their Cup a Round or two before,
And one by one crept silently to Rest.

### 22

And we, that now make merry in the Room
They left, and Summer dresses in new Bloom,
　　Ourselves must we beneath the Couch of Earth
Descend, ourselves to make a Couch—for whom?

### 23

Ah, make the most of what we yet may spend,
Before we too into the Dust descend;
　　Dust into Dust, and under Dust, to lie,
Sans Wine, sans Song, sans Singer, and—sans End!

### 24

Alike for those who for TO-DAY prepare,
And those that after a TO-MORROW stare,
　　A Muezzín from the Tower of Darkness cries
"Fools! your Reward is neither Here nor There!"

### 25

Why, all the Saints and Sages who discuss'd
Of the Two Worlds so learnedly, are thrust
   Like foolish Prophets forth; their Words to Scorn
Are scatter'd, and their Mouths are stopt with Dust.

### 26

Oh, come with old Khayyám, and leave the Wise
To talk; one thing is certain, that Life flies;
   One thing is certain, and the Rest is Lies;
The Flower that once has blown for ever dies.

### 27

Myself when young did eagerly frequent
Doctor and Saint, and heard great Argument
   About it and about: but evermore
Came out by the same Door as in I went.

### 28

With them the Seed of Wisdom did I sow,
And with my own hand labour'd it to grow:
   And this was all the Harvest that I reap'd—
"I came like Water, and like Wind I go."

**29**

Into this Universe, and *why* not knowing,
Nor *whence*, like Water willy-nilly flowing:
    And out of it, as Wind along the Waste,
I know not *whither*, willy-nilly blowing.

**30**

What, without asking, hither hurried *whence?*
And, without asking, *whither* hurried hence!
    Another and another Cup to drown
The Memory of this Impertinence!

**31**

Up from Earth's Centre through the Seventh Gate
I rose, and on the Throne of Saturn sate,
    And many Knots unravel'd by the Road;
But not the Knot of Human Death and Fate.

**32**

There was a Door to which I found no Key:
There was a Veil past which I could not see:
    Some little Talk awhile of ME and THEE
There seemed—and then no more of THEE and ME.

**33**

Then to the rolling Heav'n itself I cried,
Asking, "What Lamp had Destiny to guide
    "Her little Children stumbling in the Dark?"
And—"A blind Understanding!" Heav'n replied.


**34**

Then to this earthen Bowl did I adjourn
My Lip the secret Well of Life to learn:
    And Lip to Lip it murmur'd—"While you live
"Drink!—for once dead you never shall return."


**35**

I think the Vessel, that with fugitive
Articulation answer'd, once did live,
    And merry-make; and the cold Lip I kiss'd
How many Kisses might it take—and give!


**36**

For in the Market-place, one Dusk of Day,
I watch'd the Potter thumping his wet Clay:
    And with its all obliterated Tongue
It murmur'd—"Gently, Brother, gently, pray!"

### 37

Ah, fill the Cup:—what boots it to repeat
How Time is slipping underneath our Feet:
   Unborn TO-MORROW, and dead YESTERDAY,
Why fret about them if TO-DAY be sweet!

### 38

One Moment in Annihilation's Waste,
One Moment, of the Well of Life to taste—
   The Stars are setting and the Caravan
Starts for the Dawn of Nothing—Oh, make haste!

### 39

How long, how long, in infinite Pursuit
Of This and That endeavour and dispute?
   Better be merry with the fruitful Grape
Than sadden after none, or bitter, Fruit.

### 40

You know, my Friends, how long since in my House
For a new Marriage I did make Carouse:
   Divorced old barren Reason from my Bed,
And took the Daughter of the Vine to Spouse.

### 41

For "Is" and "Is-NOT" though *with* Rule and Line,
And "UP-AND-DOWN" *without*, I could define,
   I yet in all I only cared to know,
Was never deep in anything but—Wine.

### 42

And lately, by the Tavern Door agape,
Came stealing through the Dusk an Angel Shape
   Bearing a Vessel on his Shoulder; and
He bid me taste of it; and 'twas—the Grape!

### 43

The Grape that can with Logic absolute
The Two-and-Seventy jarring Sects confute:
   The subtle Alchemist that in a Trice
Life's leaden Metal into Gold transmute.

### 44

The mighty Mahmúd, the victorious Lord,
That all the misbelieving and black Horde
   Of Fears and Sorrows that infest the Soul
Scatters and slays with his enchanted Sword.

### 45

But leave the Wise to wrangle, and with me
The Quarrel of the Universe let be:
    And, in some corner of the Hubbub coucht,
Make Game of that which makes as much of Thee.


### 46

For in and out, above, about, below,
'Tis nothing but a Magic Shadow-show,
    Play'd in a Box whose Candle is the Sun,
Round which we Phantom Figures come and go.


### 47

And if the Wine you drink, the Lip you press,
End in the Nothing all Things end in—Yes—
    Then fancy while Thou art, Thou art but what
Thou shalt be—Nothing—Thou shalt not be less.


### 48

While the Rose blows along the River Brink,
With old Khayyám the Ruby Vintage drink:
    And when the Angel with his darker Draught
Draws up to Thee—take that, and do not shrink.

### 49

'Tis all a Chequer-board of Nights and Days
Where Destiny with Men for Pieces plays:
    Hither and thither moves, and mates, and slays,
And one by one back in the Closet lays.

### 50

The Ball no Question makes of Ayes and Noes,
But Right or Left, as strikes the Player goes;
    And He that toss'd Thee down into the Field,
*He* knows about it all—He knows—HE knows!

### 51

The Moving Finger writes; and, having writ,
Moves on: nor all thy Piety nor Wit
    Shall lure it back to cancel half a Line,
Nor all thy Tears wash out a Word of it.

### 52

And that inverted Bowl we call The Sky,
Whereunder crawling coop't we live and die,
    Lift not thy hands to *It* for help—for It
Rolls impotently on as Thou or I.

### 53

With Earth's first Clay They did the Last Man's knead,
And then of the Last Harvest sow'd the Seed:
    Yea, the first Morning of Creation wrote
What the Last Dawn of Reckoning shall read.


### 54

I tell Thee this—When, starting from the Goal,
Over the shoulders of the flaming Foal
    Of Heav'n Parwín and Mushtara they flung,
In my predestin'd Plot of Dust and Soul


### 55

The Vine had struck a Fibre; which about
If clings my Being—let the Súfi flout;
    Of my Base Metal may be filed a Key,
That shall unlock the Door he howls without


### 56

And this I know: whether the one True Light,
Kindle to Love, or Wrathconsume me quite,
    One Glimpse of It within the Tavern caught
Better than in the Temple lost outright.

## 57

Oh, Thou, who didst with Pitfall and with Gin
Beset the Road I was to wander in,
   Thou wilt not with Predestination round
Enmesh me, and impute my Fall to Sin?

## 58

Oh, Thou, who Man of baser Earth didst make,
And who with Eden didst devise the Snake;
   For all the Sin wherewith the Face of Man
Is blacken'd, Man's Forgiveness give—and take!

### KÚZA-NÁMA ("*Book of Pots.*")

## 59

Listen again. One Evening at the Close
Of Ramazán, ere the better Moon arose,
   In that old Potter's Shop I stood alone
With the clay Population round in Rows.

## 60

And, strange to tell, among that Earthen Lot
Some could articulate, while others not:
   And suddenly one more impatient cried—
"Who *is* the Potter, pray, and who the Pot?"

### 61

Then said another—"Surely not in vain
"My Substance from the common Earth was ta'en,
  "That He who subtly wrought me into Shape
"Should stamp me back to common Earth again."

### 62

Another said—"Why, ne'er a peevish Boy,
"Would break the Bowl from which he drank in Joy;
  "Shall He that *made* the Vessel in pure Love
"And Fancy, in an after Rage destroy!"

### 63

None answer'd this; but after Silence spake
A Vessel of a more ungainly Make:
  "They sneer at me for leaning all awry;
"What! did the Hand then of the Potter shake?"

### 64

Said one—"Folks of a surly Tapster tell,
"And daub his Visage with the Smoke of Hell;
  "They talk of some strict Testing of us—Pish!
"He's a Good Fellow, and 't will all be well."

### 65

Then said another with a long-drawn Sigh,
"My Clay with long oblivion is gone dry:
    "But, fill me with the old familiar Juice,
"Methinks I might recover by-and-bye!"

### 66

So while the Vessels one by one were speaking,
One spied the little Crescent all were seeking:
    And then they jogg'd each other, "Brother! Brother!
"Hark to the Porter's Shoulder-knot a-creaking!"

### 67

Ah, with the Grape my fading Life provide,
And wash my Body whence the Life has died,
    And in the Windingsheet of Vine-leaf wrapt,
So bury me by some sweet Garden-side.

### 68

That ev'n my buried Ashes such a Snare
Of Perfume shall fling up into the Air,
    As not a True Believer passing by
But shall be overtaken unaware.

### 69

Indeed the Idols I have loved so long
Have done my Credit in Men's Eye much wrong:
    Have drown'd my Honour in a shallow Cup,
And sold my Reputation for a Song.

### 70

Indeed, indeed, Repentance oft before
I swore—but was I sober when I swore?
    And then and then came Spring, and Rose-in-hand
My thread-bare Penitence apieces tore.

### 71

And much as Wine has play'd the Infidel,
And robb'd me of my Robe of Honour—well,
    I often wonder what the Vintners buy
One half so precious as the Goods they sell.

### 72

Alas, that Spring should vanish with the Rose!
That Youth's sweet-scented Manuscript should close!
    The Nightingale that in the Branches sang,
Ah, whence, and whither flown again, who knows!

### 73

Ah Love! could thou and I with Fate conspire
To grasp this sorry Scheme of Things entire,
    Would not we shatter it to bits—and then
Re-mould it nearer to the Heart's Desire!

### 74

Ah, Moon of my Delight who know'st no wane
The Moon of Heav'n is rising once again:
    How oft hereafter rising shall she look
Through this same Garden after me—in vain!

### 75

And when Thyself with shining Foot shall pass
Among the Guests Star-scatter'd on the Grass,
    And in thy joyous Errand reach the Spot
Where I made one—turn down an empty Glass!
    *TAMÁM SHUD (It is completed.)*

# Text of the
# Fifth Edition
## (*1889*)

### 1

Wake! For the Sun, who scatter'd into flight
The Stars before him from the Field of Night,
   Drives Night along with them from Heav'n, and strikes
The Sultán's Turret with a Shaft of Light.

### 2

Before the phantom of False morning died,
Methought a Voice within the Tavern cried,
   "When all the Temple is prepared within,
"Why nods the drowsy Worshipper outside?"

### 3

And, as the Cock crew, those who stood before
The Tavern shouted—"Open then the Door!
   "You know how little while we have to stay,
"And, once departed, may return no more."

### 4

Now the New Year reviving old Desires,
The thoughtful Soul to Solitude retires,
   Where the WHITE HAND OF MOSES on the Bough
Puts out, and Jesus from the Ground suspires.

### 5

Iram indeed is gone with all his Rose,
And Jamshyd's Sev'n-ring'd Cup where no one knows;
  But still a Ruby kindles in the Vine,
And many a Garden by the Water blows.

### 6

And David's Lips are lockt; but in divine
High-piping Pehleví, with "Wine! Wine! Wine!
  "Red Wine!"—the Nightingale cries to the Rose
That sallow cheek of hers to incarnadine.

### 7

Come, fill the Cup, and in the fire of Spring
Your Winter-garment of Repentance fling:
  The Bird of Time has but a little way
To flutter—and the Bird is on the Wing.

### 8

Whether at Naishápúr or Babylon,
Whether the Cup with sweet or bitter run,
  The Wine of Life keeps oozing drop by drop,
The Leaves of Life keep falling one by one.

### 9

Each Morn a thousand Roses brings, you say:
Yes, but where leaves the Rose of Yesterday?
    And this first Summer month that brings the Rose
Shall take Jamshyd and Kaikobád away.

### 10

Well, let it take them! What have we to do
With Kaikobád the Great, or Kaikhosrú?
    Let Zál and Rustum bluster as they will,
Or Hátim call to Supper—heed not you.

### 11

With me along the strip of Herbage strown
That just divides the desert from the sown,
    Where name of Slave and Sultán is forgot—
And Peace to Mahmúd on his golden Throne!

### 12

A Book of Verses underneath the Bough,
A Jug of Wine, a Loaf of Bread—and Thou
    Beside me singing in the Wilderness—
Oh, Wilderness were Paradise enow!

### 13

Some for the Glories of This World; and some
Sigh for the Prophet's Paradise to come;
    Ah, take the Cash, and let the Credit go,
Nor heed the rumble of a distant Drum!


### 14

Look to the blowing Rose about us—"Lo,
"Laughing," she says, "into the world I blow,
    "At once the silken tassel of my Purse
"Tear, and its Treasure on the Garden throw."


### 15

And those who husbanded the Golden grain,
And those who flung it to the winds like Rain,
    Alike to no such aureate Earth are turn'd
As, buried once, Men want dug up again.


### 16

The Worldly Hope men set their Hearts upon
Turns Ashes—or it prospers; and anon,
    Like Snow upon the Desert's dusty Face,
Lighting a little hour or two—is gone.

### 17

Think, in this batter'd Caravanserai
Whose Portals are alternate Night and Day,
  How Sultán after Sultán with his Pomp
Abode his destined Hour, and went his way.

### 18

They say the Lion and the Lizard keep
The Courts where Jamshyd gloried and drank deep:
  And Bahrám, that great Hunter—the Wild Ass
Stamps o'er his Head, but cannot break his Sleep.

### 19

I sometimes think that never blows so red
The Rose as where some buried Caesar bled;
  That every Hyacinth the Garden wears
Dropt in her Lap from some once lovely Head.

### 20

And this reviving Herb whose tender Green
Fledges the River-Lip on which we lean—
  Ah, lean upon it lightly! for who knows
From what once lovely Lip it springs unseen!

### 21

Ah, my Belovéd, fill the Cup that clears
To-DAY of past Regrets and future Fears:
　　*To-morrow!*—Why, To-morrow I may be
Myself with Yesterday's Sev'n thousand Years.

### 22

For some we loved, the loveliest and the best
That from his Vintage rolling Time hath prest,
　　Have drunk their Cup a Round or two before,
And one by one crept silently to rest.

### 23

And we, that now make merry in the Room
They left, and Summer dresses in new bloom,
　　Ourselves must we beneath the Couch of Earth
Descend—ourselves to make a Couch—for whom?

### 24

Ah, make the most of what we yet may spend,
Before we too into the Dust descend;
　　Dust into Dust, and under Dust to lie,
Sans Wine, sans Song, sans Singer, and—sans End!

### 25

Alike for those who for TO-DAY prepare,
And those that after some TO-MORROW stare,
    A Muezzín from the Tower of Darkness cries,
"Fools! your Reward is neither Here nor There."

### 26

Why, all the Saints and Sages who discuss'd
Of the Two Worlds so wisely—they are thrust
    Like foolish Prophets forth; their Words to Scorn
Are scatter'd, and their Mouths are stopt with Dust.

### 27

Myself when young did eagerly frequent
Doctor and Saint, and heard great argument
    About it and about: but evermore
Came out by the same door where in I went.

### 28

With them the seed of Wisdom did I sow,
And with mine own hand wrought to make it grow;
    And this was all the Harvest that I reap'd—
"I came like Water, and like Wind I go."

### 29

Into this Universe, and *Why* not knowing
Nor *Whence*, like Water willy-nilly flowing;
　　And out of it, as Wind along the Waste,
I know not *Whither*, willy-nilly blowing.

### 30

What, without asking, hither hurried *Whence?*
And, without asking, *Whither* hurried hence!
　　Oh, many a Cup of this forbidden Wine
Must drown the memory of that insolence!

### 31

Up from Earth's Centre through the Seventh Gate
I rose, and on the Throne of Saturn sate,
　　And many a Knot unravel'd by the Road;
But not the Master-knot of Human Fate.

### 32

There was the Door to which I found no Key;
There was the Veil through which I might not see:
　　Some little talk awhile of ME and THEE
There was—and then no more of THEE and ME.

### 33

Earth could not answer; nor the Seas that mourn
In flowing Purple, of their Lord forlorn;
   Nor rolling Heaven, with all his Signs reveal'd
And hidden by the sleeve of Night and Morn.

### 34

Then of the THEE IN ME who works behind
The Veil, I lifted up my hands to find
   A lamp amid the Darkness; and I heard,
As from Without—"THE ME WITHIN THEE BLIND!"

### 35

Then to the Lip of this poor earthen Urn
I lean'd, the Secret of my Life to learn:
   And Lip to Lip it murmur'd—"While you live,
"Drink!—for, once dead, you never shall return."

### 36

I think the Vessel, that with fugitive
Articulation answer'd, once did live,
   And drink; and Ah! the passive Lip I kiss'd,
How many Kisses might it take—and give!

**37**

For I remember stopping by the way
To watch a Potter thumping his wet Clay:
   And with its all-obliterated Tongue
It murmur'd—"Gently, Brother, gently, pray!"

**38**

And has not such a Story from of Old
Down Man's successive generations roll'd
   Of such a clod of saturated Earth
Cast by the Maker into Human mould?

**39**

And not a drop that from our Cups we throw
For Earth to drink of, but may steal below
   To quench the fire of Anguish in some Eye
There hidden—far beneath, and long ago.

**40**

As then the Tulip for her morning sup
Of Heav'nly Vintage from the soil looks up,
   Do you devoutly do the like, till Heav'n
To Earth invert you—like an empty Cup.

**41**

Perplext no more with Human or Divine,
To-morrow's tangle to the winds resign,
   And lose your fingers in the tresses of
The Cypress-slender Minister of Wine.


**42**

And if the Wine you drink, the Lip you press,
End in what All begins and ends in—Yes;
   Think then you are TO-DAY what YESTERDAY
You were—TO-MORROW you shall not be less.


**43**

So when that Angel of the darker Drink
At last shall find you by the river-brink,
   And, offering his Cup, invite your Soul
Forth to your Lips to quaff—you shall not shrink.


**44**

Why, if the Soul can fling the Dust aside,
And naked on the Air of Heaven ride,
   Were't not a Shame—were't not a Shame for him
In this clay carcase crippled to abide?

### 45

'Tis but a Tent where takes his one day's rest
A Sultán to the realm of Death addrest;
    The Sultán rises, and the dark Ferrásh
Strikes, and prepares it for another Guest.

### 46

And fear not lest Existence closing your
Account, and mine, should know the like no more;
    The Eternal Sákí from that Bowl has pour'd
Millions of Bubbles like us, and will pour.

### 47

When You and I behind the Veil are past,
Oh, but the long, long while the World shall last,
    Which of our Coming and Departure heeds
As the Sea's self should heed a pebble-cast.

### 48

A Moment's Halt—a momentary taste
Of BEING from the Well amid the Waste—
    And Lo!—the phantom Caravan has reach'd
The NOTHING it set out from—Oh, make haste!

### 49

Would you that spangle of Existence spend
About THE SECRET—quick about it, Friend!
   A Hair perhaps divides the False and True—
And upon what, prithee, may life depend?

### 50

A Hair perhaps divides the False and True;
Yes; and a single Alif were the clue—
   Could you but find it—to the Treasure-house,
And peradventure to THE MASTER too;

### 51

Whose secret Presence, through Creation's veins
Running Quicksilver-like eludes your pains;
   Taking all shapes from Máh to Máhi; and
They change and perish all—but He remains;

### 52

A moment guess'd—then back behind the Fold
Immerst of Darkness round the Drama roll'd
   Which, for the Pastime of Eternity,
He doth Himself contrive, enact, behold.

### 53

But if in vain, down on the stubborn floor
Of Earth, and up to Heav'n's unopening Door
    You gaze TO-DAY, while You are You—how then
TO-MORROW, when You shall be You no more?

### 54

Waste not your Hour, nor in the vain pursuit
Of This and That endeavour and dispute;
    Better be jocund with the fruitful Grape
Than sadden after none, or bitter, Fruit.

### 55

You know, my Friends, with what a brave Carouse
I made a Second Marriage in my house;
    Divorced old barren Reason from my Bed,
And took the Daughter of the Vine to Spouse.

### 56

For "Is" and "Is-NOT" though with Rule and Line
And "UP-AND-DOWN" by Logic I define,
    Of all that one should care to fathom, I
Was never deep in anything but—Wine.

### 57

Ah, but my Computations, People say,
Reduced the Year to better reckoning?—Nay,
   'Twas only striking from the Calendar
Unborn To-morrow and dead Yesterday.

### 58

And lately, by the Tavern Door agape,
Came shining through the Dusk an Angel Shape
   Bearing a Vessel on his Shoulder; and
He bid me taste of it; and 'twas—the Grape!

### 59

The Grape that can with Logic absolute
The Two-and-Seventy jarring Sects confute:
   The sovereign Alchemist that in a trice
Life's leaden metal into Gold transmute:

### 60

The mighty Mahmúd, Allah-breathing Lord,
That all the misbelieving and black Horde
   Of Fears and Sorrows that infest the Soul
Scatters before him with his whirlwind Sword.

### 61

Why, be this Juice the growth of God, who dare
Blaspheme the twisted tendril as a Snare?

    A Blessing, we should use it, should we not?
And if a Curse—why, then, who set it there?

### 62

I must abjure the Balm of Life, I must,
Scared by some After-reckoning ta'en on trust,

    Or lured with Hope of some Diviner Drink,
To fill the Cup—when crumbled into Dust!

### 63

Oh threats of Hell and Hopes of Paradise!
One thing at least is certain—*This* Life flies;

    One thing is certain and the rest is Lies;
The Flower that once has blown for ever dies.

### 64

Strange, is it not? that of the myriads who
Before us pass'd the door of Darkness through,

    Not one returns to tell us of the Road,
Which to discover we must travel too.

### 65

The Revelations of Devout and Learn'd
Who rose before us, and as Prophets burn'd,
   Are all but Stories, which, awoke from Sleep
They told their comrades, and to Sleep return'd.

### 66

I sent my Soul through the Invisible,
Some Letter of that After-life to spell:
   And by and by my Soul return'd to me,
And answer'd "I Myself am Heav'n and Hell:"

### 67

Heav'n but the Vision of fulfill'd Desire,
And Hell the Shadow from a Soul on fire,
   Cast on the Darkness into which Ourselves,
So late emerged from, shall so soon expire.

### 68

We are no other than a moving row
Of Magic Shadow-shapes that come and go
   Round with the Sun-illumined Lantern held
In Midnight by the Master of the Show;

### 69

But helpless Pieces of the Game He plays
Upon this Chequer-board of Nights and Days;
   Hither and thither moves, and checks, and slays,
And one by one back in the Closet lays.

### 70

The Ball no question makes of Ayes and Noes,
But Here or There as strikes the Player goes;
   And He that toss'd you down into the Field,
*He* knows about it all—HE knows—HE knows!

### 71

The Moving Finger writes; and, having writ,
Moves on: nor all your Piety nor Wit
   Shall lure it back to cancel half a Line,
Nor all your Tears wash out a Word of it.

### 72

And that inverted Bowl they call the Sky,
Whereunder crawling coop'd we live and die,
   Lift not your hands to *It* for help—for It
As impotently moves as you or I.

### 73

With Earth's first Clay They did the Last Man knead,
And there of the Last Harvest sow'd the Seed:
    And the first Morning of Creation wrote
What the Last Dawn of Reckoning shall read.


### 74

YESTERDAY *This* Day's Madness did prepare;
TOMORROW's Silence, Triumph, or Despair:
    Drink! for you know not whence you came, nor why:
Drink! for you know not why you go, nor where.


### 75

I tell you this—When, started from the Goal,
Over the flaming shoulders of the Foal
    Of Heav'n Parwín and Mushtarí they flung,
In my predestined Plot of Dust and Soul


### 76

The Vine had struck a fibre: which about
If clings my Being—let the Dervish flout;
    Of my Base metal may be filed a Key
That shall unlock the Door he howls without.

### 77

And this I know: whether the one True Light
Kindle to Love, or Wrath-consume me quite,
  One Flash of It within the Tavern caught
Better than in the Temple lost outright.

### 78

What! out of senseless Nothing to provoke
A conscious Something to resent the yoke
  Of unpermitted Pleasure, under pain
Of Everlasting Penalties, if broke!

### 79

What! from his helpless Creature be repaid
Pure Gold for what he lent him dross-allay'd—
  Sue for a Debt he never did contract,
And cannot answer—Oh the sorry trade!

### 80

Oh Thou, who didst with pitfall and with gin
Beset the Road I was to wander in,
  Thou wilt not with Predestined Evil round
Enmesh, and then impute my Fall to Sin!

### 81

Oh Thou, who Man of baser Earth didst make,
And ev'n with Paradise devise the Snake:
    For all the Sin wherewith the Face of Man
Is blacken'd—Man's forgiveness give—and take!

\* \* \* \* \* \* \*

### 82

As under cover of departing Day
Slunk hunger-stricken Ramazán away,
    Once more within the Potter's house alone
I stood, surrounded by the Shapes of Clay.

### 83

Shapes of all Sorts and Sizes, great and small,
That stood along the floor and by the wall;
    And some loquacious Vessels were; and some
Listen'd perhaps, but never talk'd at all.

### 84

Said one among them—"Surely not in vain
"My substance of the common Earth was ta'en
    "And to this Figure moulded, to be broke,
"Or trampled back to shapeless Earth again."

### 85

Then said a Second—"Ne'er a peevish Boy
"Would break the Bowl from which he drank in joy;
   "And He that with his hand the Vessel made
"Will surely not in after Wrath destroy."

### 86

After a momentary silence spake
Some Vessel of a more ungainly Make;
   "They sneer at me for leaning all awry:
"What! did the Hand then of the Potter shake?"

### 87

Whereat some one of the loquacious Lot—
I think a Súfi pipkin—waxing hot—
   "All this of Pot and Potter—Tell me, then,
"Who is the Potter, pray, and who the Pot?"

### 88

"Why," said another, "Some there are who tell
"Of one who threatens he will toss to Hell
   "The luckless Pots he marr'd in making—Pish!
"He's a Good Fellow, and 't will all be well."

## 89

"Well," murmur'd one, "Let whoso make or buy,
"My Clay with long Oblivion is gone dry:
    "But fill me with the old familiar Juice,
"Methinks I might recover by and by."

## 90

So while the Vessels one by one were speaking,
The little Moon look'd in that all were seeking:
    And then they jogg'd each other, "Brother! Brother!
"Now for the Porter's shoulder-knot a-creaking!"

## 91

Ah, with the Grape my fading life provide,
And wash the Body whence the Life has died,
    And lay me, shrouded in the living Leaf,
By some not unfrequented Garden-side.

## 92

That ev'n my buried Ashes such a snare
Of Vintage shall fling up into the Air
    As not a True-believer passing by
But shall be overtaken unaware.

### 93

Indeed the Idols I have loved so long
Have done my credit in this World much wrong:
    Have drown'd my Glory in a shallow Cup,
And sold my Reputation for a Song.

### 94

Indeed, indeed, Repentance oft before
I swore—but was I sober when I swore?
    And then and then came Spring, and Rose-in-hand
My thread-bare Penitence apieces tore.

### 95

And much as Wine has play'd the Infidel,
And robb'd me of my Robe of Honour—Well,
    I wonder often what the Vintners buy
One half so precious as the stuff they sell.

### 96

Yet Ah, that Spring should vanish with the Rose!
That Youth's sweet-scented manuscript should close!
    The Nightingale that in the branches sang,
Ah whence, and whither flown again, who knows!

### 97

Would but the Desert of the Fountain yield
One glimpse—if dimly, yet indeed, reveal'd,
  To which the fainting Traveller might spring,
As springs the trampled herbage of the field!

### 98

Would but some wingéd Angel ere too late
Arrest the yet unfolded Roll of Fate,
  And make the stern Recorder otherwise
Enregister, or quite obliterate!

### 99

Ah Love! could you and I with Him conspire
To grasp this sorry Scheme of Things entire,
  Would not we shatter it to bits—and then
Re-mould it nearer to the Heart's Desire!

### 100

Yon rising Moon that looks for us again—
How oft hereafter will she wax and wane;
  How oft hereafter rising look for us
Through this same Garden—and for *one* in vain

### 101

And when like her, oh Sákí, you shall pass
Among the Guests Star-scatter'd on the Grass,
   And in your joyous errand reach the spot
Where I made One—turn down an empty Glass!
          *TAMÁM*

# Notes

## FIRST EDITION

STANZA NO.

1. "flung the Stone" refers to flinging a stone into a cup as a signal for departure.
2. "Dawn's Left Hand": pre-dawn light in the sky.
4. "White Hand of Moses," alluding to Moses' leprous hand in the Bible, here refers to spring blossoms.
5. Irám: legendary ancient garden. Jamshýd: legendary Persian king credited with introducing civilized arts to mankind.
6. Péhlevi: Middle Persian, the form of the language from the third to tenth centuries A.D.
8, 9. Kaikobád and Kaikhosrú: two of the legendary Persian kings in the great national epic, the *Shahnamah* (completed 1011). Rustum: chief hero of that epic. Hátim Tai: legendary hospitable Arab.
10. Máhmúd (of Ghazna): great conqueror and patron of the author of the *Shahnamah*, Firdausi.
16. Caravanserai: inn for merchants and travelers.
17. Bahrám (Gur): legendary king in the *Shahnamah*, renowned as a hunter.
24. Muezzín: caller to prayer.
50. "The Ball": in the game of polo, invented in Persia or Central Asia.
54. Foal of Heav'n, Parwín, Mushtara: various constellations and heavenly bodies.
55. Súfi: Islamic mystic.
59. Ramazán: month of daytime fasting.
66. "Crescent": the first welcome glimpse of the new moon ending the month of fasting.

## FIFTH EDITION

2. "phantom of False morning": same as "Dawn's Left Hand" in the first edition.
8. Naishápúr: Nishapur, birthplace of Omar Khayyam in northeastern Persia.

9. Zál: hero in the *Shahnamah*, father of Rustum.
45. Ferrásh: servant.
46. Sákí: cupbearer.
50. Alif: first letter of the Arabic alphabet, a single vertical stroke.
51. Máh: Persian for moon. Máhi: Persian for fish.

# DOVER · THRIFT · EDITIONS

All books complete and unabridged. All 5³⁄₁₆" × 8¼", paperbound.
Just $1.00–$2.00 in U.S.A.

## POETRY

GREAT LOVE POEMS, Shane Weller (ed.). 128pp. 27284-2 $1.00

SELECTED POEMS, Walt Whitman. 128pp. 26878-0 $1.00

THE BALLAD OF READING GAOL AND OTHER POEMS, Oscar Wilde. 64pp. 27072-6 $1.00

FAVORITE POEMS, William Wordsworth. 80pp. 27073-4 $1.00

EARLY POEMS, William Butler Yeats. 128pp. 27808-5 $1.00

## FICTION

FLATLAND: A ROMANCE OF MANY DIMENSIONS, Edwin A. Abbott. 96pp. 27263-X $1.00

BEOWULF, Beowulf (trans. by R. K. Gordon). 64pp. 27264-8 $1.00

CIVIL WAR STORIES, Ambrose Bierce. 128pp. 28038-1 $1.00

ALICE'S ADVENTURES IN WONDERLAND, Lewis Carroll. 96pp. 27543-4 $1.00

O PIONEERS!, Willa Cather. 128pp. 27785-2 $1.00

FIVE GREAT SHORT STORIES, Anton Chekhov. 96pp. 26463-7 $1.00

FAVORITE FATHER BROWN STORIES, G. K. Chesterton. 96pp. 27545-0 $1.00

THE AWAKENING, Kate Chopin. 128pp. 27786-0 $1.00

HEART OF DARKNESS, Joseph Conrad. 80pp. 26464-5 $1.00

THE SECRET SHARER AND OTHER STORIES, Joseph Conrad. 128pp. 27546-9 $1.00

THE OPEN BOAT AND OTHER STORIES, Stephen Crane. 128pp. 27547-7 $1.00

THE RED BADGE OF COURAGE, Stephen Crane. 112pp. 26465-3 $1.00

A CHRISTMAS CAROL, Charles Dickens. 80pp. 26865-9 $1.00

THE CRICKET ON THE HEARTH AND OTHER CHRISTMAS STORIES, Charles Dickens. 128pp. 28039-X $1.00

NOTES FROM THE UNDERGROUND, Fyodor Dostoyevsky. 96pp. 27053-X $1.00

SIX GREAT SHERLOCK HOLMES STORIES, Sir Arthur Conan Doyle. 112pp. 27055-6 $1.00

WHERE ANGELS FEAR TO TREAD, E. M. Forster. 128pp. (Available in U.S. only) 27791-7 $1.00

THE OVERCOAT AND OTHER SHORT STORIES, Nikolai Gogol. 112pp. 27057-2 $1.00

GREAT GHOST STORIES, John Grafton (ed.). 112pp. 27270-2 $1.00

THE LUCK OF ROARING CAMP AND OTHER SHORT STORIES, Bret Harte. 96pp. 27271-0 $1.00

THE SCARLET LETTER, Nathaniel Hawthorne. 192pp. 28048-9 $2.00

YOUNG GOODMAN BROWN AND OTHER SHORT STORIES, Nathaniel Hawthorne. 128pp. 27060-2 $1.00

THE GIFT OF THE MAGI AND OTHER SHORT STORIES, O. Henry. 96pp. 27061-0 $1.00

THE NUTCRACKER AND THE GOLDEN POT, E. T. A. Hoffmann. 128pp. 27806-9 $1.00

THE BEAST IN THE JUNGLE AND OTHER STORIES, Henry James. 128pp. 27552-3 $1.00

THE TURN OF THE SCREW, Henry James. 96pp. 26684-2 $1.00

DUBLINERS, James Joyce. 160pp. 26870-5 $1.00

A PORTRAIT OF THE ARTIST AS A YOUNG MAN, James Joyce. 192pp. 28050-0 $2.00

# DOVER · THRIFT · EDITIONS

All books complete and unabridged. All 5³⁄₁₆″ × 8¼″, paperbound.
Just $1.00–$2.00 in U.S.A.

## FICTION

THE MAN WHO WOULD BE KING AND OTHER STORIES, Rudyard Kipling. 128pp. 28051-9
$1.00

SELECTED SHORT STORIES, D. H. Lawrence. 128pp. 27794-1 $1.00

GREEN TEA AND OTHER GHOST STORIES, J. Sheridan LeFanu. 96pp. 27795-X $1.00

THE CALL OF THE WILD, Jack London. 64pp. 26472-6 $1.00

FIVE GREAT SHORT STORIES, Jack London. 96pp. 27063-7 $1.00

WHITE FANG, Jack London. 160pp. 26968-X $1.00

THE NECKLACE AND OTHER SHORT STORIES, Guy de Maupassant. 128pp. 27064-5 $1.00

BARTLEBY AND BENITO CERENO, Herman Melville. 112pp. 26473-4 $1.00

THE GOLD-BUG AND OTHER TALES, Edgar Allan Poe. 128pp. 26875-6 $1.00

THE QUEEN OF SPADES AND OTHER STORIES, Alexander Pushkin. 128pp. 28054-3 $1.00

THREE LIVES, Gertrude Stein. 176pp. 28059-4 $2.00

THE STRANGE CASE OF DR. JEKYLL AND MR. HYDE, Robert Louis Stevenson. 64pp.
26688-5 $1.00

TREASURE ISLAND, Robert Louis Stevenson. 160pp. 27559-0 $1.00

THE KREUTZER SONATA AND OTHER SHORT STORIES, Leo Tolstoy. 144pp. 27805-0 $1.00

ADVENTURES OF HUCKLEBERRY FINN, Mark Twain. 224pp. 28061-6 $2.00

THE MYSTERIOUS STRANGER AND OTHER STORIES, Mark Twain. 128pp. 27069-6 $1.00

CANDIDE, Voltaire (François-Marie Arouet). 112pp. 26689-3 $1.00

THE INVISIBLE MAN, H. G. Wells. 112pp. (Available in U.S. only.) 27071-8 $1.00

ETHAN FROME, Edith Wharton. 96pp. 26690-7 $1.00

THE PICTURE OF DORIAN GRAY, Oscar Wilde. 192pp. 27807-7 $1.00

## NONFICTION

THE DEVIL'S DICTIONARY, Ambrose Bierce. 144pp. 27542-6 $1.00

THE SOULS OF BLACK FOLK, W. E. B. Du Bois. 176pp. 28041-1 $2.00

SELF-RELIANCE AND OTHER ESSAYS, Ralph Waldo Emerson. 128pp. 27790-9 $1.00

GREAT SPEECHES, Abraham Lincoln. 112pp. 26872-1 $1.00

THE PRINCE, Niccolò Machiavelli. 80pp. 27274-5 $1.00

SYMPOSIUM AND PHAEDRUS, Plato. 96pp. 27798-4 $1.00

THE TRIAL AND DEATH OF SOCRATES: FOUR DIALOGUES, Plato. 128pp. 27066-1 $1.00

CIVIL DISOBEDIENCE AND OTHER ESSAYS, Henry David Thoreau. 96pp. 27563-9 $1.00

THE THEORY OF THE LEISURE CLASS, Thorstein Veblen. 256pp. 28062-4 $2.00

## PLAYS

THE CHERRY ORCHARD, Anton Chekhov. 64pp. 26682-6 $1.00

THE THREE SISTERS, Anton Chekhov. 64pp. 27544-2 $1.00

THE WAY OF THE WORLD, William Congreve. 80pp. 27787-9 $1.00

MEDEA, Euripides. 64pp. 27548-5 $1.00

THE MIKADO, William Schwenck Gilbert. 64pp. 27268-0 $1.00